BETWEEN A ROCK AND A HARD PLACE

A Report on School Worship

ALAN BROWN

Published on behalf of the General Synod Board of Education by The National Society (Church of England) for Promoting Religious Education

ISBN 0 901819 46 8

Copyright © The National Society (Church of England) for Promoting Religious Education 1996. This publication may not be reproduced, either in whole or in part, whether for sale or otherwise, without written permission which should be sought from The National Society, Church House, Great Smith Street, London SW1P 3NZ.

Printed by Bourne Press Limited, Bournemouth

Contents

Preface by the Rt Revd the Lord Bishop of Ripon		v
1	Introduction	1
2	Responses from Diocesan Boards of Education	6
3	Collective School Worship Seminars	19
4	Conclusion	29
5	The Board of Education – A Policy Statement: School Worship	34
Appendix A:	School Worship Seminars: Those Invited to Attend	37
Appendix B:	School Worship Seminars: Those Expected to Attend	39
Appendix C:	School Worship: Invitation from the Board of Education	43
Appendix D:	An Extract from the CJEPC Working Party Document on Collective Worship	45

Preface

One of the more remarkable features of the progress of the Education Reform Bills through Parliament in 1987–88 was that debates on religious education and collective worship provided more column inches in Hansard than any other single subject. Today, eight years on, school worship is no less controversial; the flames have been fanned by Circular 1/94 on 'Religious education and collective worship' and the OFSTED inspection of school worship itself.

The Board of Education of the General Synod, weighing carefully the issues in the debate before arriving at its own policy on collective worship, decided to consult widely among Diocesan Boards of Education. In addition, the St Gabriel's Trust generously enabled a series of seminars to be held in which various interested parties had every opportunity to express an opinion. Virtually every diocesan board responded and over one hundred people attended the seminars, making the consultation one of the most comprehensive undertaken by the Board in recent years.

The Report makes interesting reading and, together with the Board's agreed policy on school worship, provides a helpful and supportive framework for teachers leading worship and headteachers responsible for its organisation and administration.

Thanks are due to the St Gabriel's Trust and the Diocesan Boards of Education for their support, financial and otherwise. Julia Jones, Administrator of the National Society's RE Centre who organised the seminars, booked the venues, ensured papers were sent out and typed (and re-typed) the final manuscript, also deserves our thanks and gratitude.

The Rt Revd the Lord Bishop of Ripon
Chairman of the General Synod Board of Education
December 1995

1

Introduction

Just before the publication of the Education Reform Bill in 1987 the (then) Department of Education and Science invited a number of interested organisations to express an opinion on the current situation regarding school worship.

After considerable discussion the Board of Education agreed a policy which questioned the rightness and practicability of the daily requirement for collective school worship (as did the Free Church Federal Council) and advocated a change in the law which would no longer require county schools to hold an act of worship for all pupils every day, although there should be a regular pattern of worship in the school week. The subsequent legislation in the Education Reform Act 1988, introduced into the House of Lords by the then Chairman of the Board of Education in a parliamentary debate that made it clear that the Government would not be prepared to end the daily requirement, re-affirmed the importance of the daily act of collective worship but allowed greater flexibility than had previously been required by the 1944 Education Act. An indication of the central focus of collective school worship was also given.

The law now allowed schools to meet for collective worship in small groups and at any time of the day; the age, aptitude and family background of the pupils had to be borne in mind; Christian acts of collective school worship should take place on the majority of days in any one term (these were defined as 'acts of a wholly or mainly broadly Christian character' and did give rise, with other parts of that Act, to a variety of tortuous expositions of what had been intended); and enabled determinations to be sought by schools where it was deemed impossible or unrealistic to meet the 'Christian' requirement.

The furore over the worship requirements of the Act settled down. One Religious Education Adviser in 1988 prophesied 10,000 determinations but, as expected, under 300 schools have been granted determinations, with the vast majority of them coming from four or five Local Education Authorities.

In fact the immediate consequence of the Act was the production of a great deal of material intended to support schools in the conduct of collective worship. A large number of LEAs produced policies on school worship in county schools together with advice, guidance and resources. The Churches too, worked with LEAs in both Standing Advisory Councils on Religious Education (SACRES) and through their own networks to provide advice and support. It is perhaps one of the most overlooked features of the consequences of the Education Reform Act that a whole 'school worship' industry grew up almost overnight. Sales of books for school worship boomed and continue apace.

Two events then occurred which caused those responsible for worship in schools to reflect.

The two events were:

(i) the change in inspection arrangements and the creation of the Office for Standards in Education (OFSTED) and

(ii) the publication of Circular 1/94 'Religious education and collective worship'.

The inspection process

As a result of the introduction of the four-yearly cycle of inspections in 1993, the true pattern of schools' compliance with the daily requirement for school worship would become apparent for the first time. Inspectors were required to note whether the schools inspected were obeying the law in this regard. Schools which had either ignored the law or paid lip-service to it would be easily identified; so would schools which had tried to maintain the spirit of the law but failed to keep the law to the letter.

Establishing the legality of a school's policy on collective worship had never been easy because there were no agreed criteria about what constituted an act of collective worship. Inspectors themselves may disagree about whether an observed act of collective worship is indeed an act of collective worship! Were there specific ingredients which had to be present? When was an assembly purporting to be an act of worship not an act of worship? So inspectors needed to be clear about the definite content of collective school worship.

The other issue for inspectors was the link between collective school worship and one of the core elements in school inspections, that of the inspection of the spiritual, moral, social and cultural (SMSC) development of pupils. In practice, a school which might not address the letter of the law regarding collective worship could provide excellent opportunities for the pupils' spiritual, moral, social and cultural development. Some schools, recognising the difficulty of meeting the daily legal requirement, have compensated for this by ensuring opportunities are provided for pupils' SMSC development and this is clearly stated in their policies. It may be necessary to draw attention to such schools for breaking the daily requirement but (a) the breaking of the requirement has to be set in the context of the whole school provision, and (b) it would not necessarily enhance the SMSC provision for pupils if the daily provision were met.

As a result of two years of the inspection of secondary schools and one year of primary schools, it appears the vast majority of primary schools (c 85%) do keep the daily requirement whereas only c 20% of secondary schools do. (These figures include the denominational schools.)

DFE Circular 1/94 (10/94 as issued by the Welsh Office)

The confusion over the meaning and intention of the Education Reform Act had begun to settle and, as referred to earlier, many LEAs and religious bodies had responded to the needs of schools. The publication of Circular 1/94 (and its consultative predecessor X/94) 'Religious education and collective worship' raised anxieties of those who had believed the words of the Bishop of London and Baroness Hooper in the House of Lords in 1988 when they said that the flexibility in the provisions for school worship written into the Education Reform Act would encourage, support and enable the great majority of school communities to worship together.

It will be necessary to return to the detail of Circular 1/94 later but here it is sufficient to note its three central areas of controversy:

(i)   it provided a definition of worship;

(ii) it defined an act of Christian collective worship as one in which attention was accorded to the special status of Jesus Christ;

(iii) it indicated that all pupils should be able to participate in some way.

These interpretations of the law caused unease among Christian teachers and non-teachers, members of other faith traditions, and among a large number of teachers who had been able to participate and lead school worship now felt compromised by the Government's interpretation of the law. The legal advice sought by the Board of Deputies of British Jews went so far as to state that the interpretation of the law was 'outwith the Act'.

The deep concern over the wording of the Circular 1/94 not only built upon the fears created by the new style of inspection but was compounded when OFSTED appeared to accept and use the criteria of Circular 1/94 in the advice for inspecting collective worship in its Schools Update 9. Whereas the original wording of the Education Reform Act, together with the views of many who spoke in favour of it, had allowed some controlled flexibility for schools and a freedom to build upon advice and guidance, it now appeared that a pincer movement between OFSTED and Circular 1/94 was cutting out that flexibility and making demands of schools, teachers and pupils which the law had not intended.

The Board of Education

In the meantime the Board of Education had amended its policy from one which did not support the legislation to one which accepted current legal requirements and recognised that the main duty of the Board and diocesan officers was to support schools and those responsible for the organisation, administration and presentation of collective school worship.

In one of its responses to the (then) DFE (in 1993) the Board pointed out that for the majority of pupils the only acts of worship they would normally attend were those held in school and suggested that it might be helpful, given appropriate parental approval, for pupils to see a corporate act of worship if they were to gain a real and deeper insight into the importance of worship for a believer. This opinion was criticised by some, including MPs in the House of Commons, but it did raise the dilemma of how pupils are to understand the meaning, purpose and depth of worship if they only experience low quality, perfunctory opportunities for collective worship in schools.

At its meeting in the Autumn of 1994 the Board, with the valuable assistance of the St Gabriel's In-Service Programme, decided to hold a series of seminars in 1995 to which would be invited various organisations who had an interest in collective school worship (see Appendix A for the full list). The organisations which responded were invited to send members to one of the five seminars, and the list of those who expressed a wish to attend are included in Appendix B. The Board was pleased that OFSTED could be represented although the lack of representation from the School Curriculum and Assessment Authority and the (then) DFE was a disappointment.

The Board also invited the Diocesan Boards of Education to discuss the issue. A number of questions were drawn up and sent to the Boards. The questions asked are in Appendix C.

This was a very comprehensive exercise, certainly the largest on the issue of collective school worship in the recent history of the Board, and the concerns and conclusions of the DBEs and seminars are set out below.

The Board has been involved in the consultative procedures of the Church Joint Education Policy Committee (CJEPC) which has also taken an initiative on collective school worship, seeking to provide an ecumenical response to the situation. The CJEPC paper was sent out to all those who attended the seminars and the Board's reflections on school worship will form part of its response to that document (cf. Appendix D).

2
Responses from Diocesan Boards of Education

hirty-eight dioceses returned written responses to the General Synod's Board of Education. The responses to each question are summarised in turn.

> The law requires every maintained school to provide a daily act of collective worship for every pupil registered at the school (unless withdrawn by parental request). Would the Diocesan Board of Education agree with the law as it stands or press for a change? What is the rationale for its opinion on this issue?

Of those thirty-eight Diocesan Boards, four did not wish there to be a change in the law though there was a recognition that the current situation is far from satisfactory. Five DBE's said that there was no real problem with the daily act of collective worship in primary schools but the situation with regard to secondary schools needed attention and greater flexibility (i.e. a change in the law). Twenty-nine DBEs expressed a concern over the inadequacy of the law for many schools, particularly secondary schools, and stated clearly that there did need to be a change in the law. However, there was no clear or unanimous advice about what, if anything, should be put in its place. Some reverted to a version of the GS Board of Education's earlier policy that there should be a 'pattern' of worship in the week with a minimum of two or three acts of worship; others felt that as county primary schools appeared to be meeting the legal requirement there should only be a change for secondary schools.

All DBEs were concerned that collective school worship should remain part of school life. All were concerned to reaffirm their commitment to daily worship in voluntary and grant maintained church schools although again, there was a recognition that some Church secondary schools had a problem if the daily requirement was to be met rigorously.

Some responses made it clear that the DBE was not unanimous in its conclusion and felt uncomfortable having to make any recommendations. One Diocesan Board suggested that while there should be a limited change in the law, there should be safeguards, perhaps using SACRES, to ensure that greater flexibility did not allow abuse of the law. Another diocese, remarking that the law is not helpful, stated openly that there was 'fear of change' as it was not sure what the consequences of any change in the law might be. Interestingly, only one DBE argued in favour of a revision of the law based on the belief that it is inappropriate to require pupils to worship in schools which have no religious foundation. This view was expressed frequently in the seminars but the DBEs – even though some members obviously supported the view – still would not be in favour of the abolition of collective school worship.

A recurring theme, which will also be touched upon later, was the very narrow 'definition' of worship made available to schools. Some DBE's felt that the narrower or more limited definition of worship, made it more important for the intended flexibility of the legislation to be revisited. Schools had to be allowed some flexibility and if this was removed then there would inevitably be pressure to change the law.

Summary

(i) A great majority were in favour of some changes in the law on the frequency of collective worship to allow greater flexibility, particularly for secondary schools.

(ii) In principle, worship should continue to be daily in all church schools although many diocesan boards would welcome greater flexibility.

(iii) Any change in the daily requirement should be accompanied by a broader and more flexible definition of worship.

How best can schools meet the needs of the challenge of conducting daily worship in schools in a multi-faith/no faith community?

DBEs responded to this question in different ways. For some dioceses the question is not an issue either because within the diocese there are few members of other faith communities or because the multi-faith/no faith issue has not created any controversy. In this context it is interesting that one DBE, which has few members of other faiths in its own diocese, wrote:

> Amend Section 7 of the Education (Reform) Act 1988 so as to require an act which recognises the duty to promote the spiritual and moral development of pupils, but which permits that duty to be interpreted in a way appropriate for the pupils bearing in mind their family backgrounds, ages and aptitudes. Thus it would be permissible for an act of worship to be wholly or mainly of a broadly Christian, broadly Muslim, Jewish, Buddhist, Hindu or Sikh character, whatever is appropriate.

Another response touches the feelings of some others when it states:

> The testimony of an evangelical head teacher working in a school serving a multi-faith community is that spirituality from within encompasses all faiths, and all can comfortably share in stillness, silence and reflection.

The last three words recur in a number of diocesan responses along with 'sensitivity', 'respect', 'a sense of the numinous', 'listening' and 'shared beliefs, values and morals'.

One diocese notes that exploring worship, in the context of a multi-faith school (or even in any context) is a 'curious contradiction'. Another suggests schools would be better devising 'occasions that would be of positive benefit for all pupils and staff'.

An optimistic and positive attitude towards the possibilities of collective school worship comes with one response:

> The challenge of providing collective worship which reflects the broad traditions of Christian belief has been taken up by many county primary schools. Where INSET has been provided which acknowledges the richness of faith within a whole school community and where collective worship is planned to be inclusive, pupils' experiences are positive ones.

One might not disagree with the sentiment or the ideal, but the judgement of positive experiences is a difficult one to make. Certainly, however, the word 'inclusive' is commonly found in the responses. One DBE takes a rather different view:

> It is strange that many headteachers place a rather spurious unity (having the whole school together) above meaningful and honest worship, which may require that on occasions there are separate services for, say,

Christians (and nominal adherents) and practising Moslems. For young people it is surely better to have separate acts of worship which are real than to have no opportunity to worship at all, merely some moralising.

One DBE indicated the diversity of its opinion by recording the views of 'Groups A and B'. Both views are important to be heard as they reflect the complexity of any attempt to resolve a very difficult issue:

Group A

The experience of this group is that a multi-faith community is no serious obstacle to a daily act of worship, even when this is Christian worship and would further challenge that the no-faith community exists to the extent that your question suggests. In schools where there is a significant number of believing but non-Christian pupils the suggestion is to provide an act of worship suited to their religion on a withdrawal basis.

Group B

Would suggest that to best support those working in a multi-faith/no faith situation either the word 'worship' be interpreted more flexibly or the word not be used at all... It is not that schools do not wish to meet together for communal purposes and to promote and hold commonly agreed values such as love, truthfulness, honesty, forgiveness, kindness, etc it is rather that many who work in schools, staff and pupils, are extremely uncomfortable with the word and the concept of worship and its implications.

Only two responses spent much time on the no-faith aspect of the question or as they phrased it, 'where the local population is only distantly connected with the church'. After making a general point (also made by others) about the value of in-service training and linking pupils' spiritual development to the whole curriculum, one statement continues:

> But it is perhaps important to say that the Church can only help schools if it is trusted not to use the opportunities offered for its own evangelising purposes. It is crucial to take seriously the secular stance of teachers and schools and to work within the integrity of those who are legally bound to provide acts of worship, despite their own viewpoint.

The other response states:

> If by 'no-faith' is meant 'entirely secular' then there is every reason that the philosophy of collective worship should be broadly conceived in educationally hospitable terms so that no pupil – or adult – should feel excluded.

One DBE captured the flavour of the concern of many by drawing a distinction between 'worship' in its 'natural and ordinary meaning' (Circular 1/94, para. 57) and a broader sense caught by the word 'collective' which recognises 'that pupils come from a wide range of religious and non-religious backgrounds, which makes 'corporate' impossible'.

> Worship, in both its natural and ordinary sense and in a broader sense, is clearly distinct from other school activities whilst being related to them. What is distinctive about worship is the extent to which it provides opportunities for pupils to:
>
> *affirm* some value of ultimate worth which, for some, will be God;
>
> *celebrate* in songs, hymns, readings and other ways;
>
> *respond* collectively and individually through statements of belief, prayer, silence or reflection.

Summary

(i) It is difficult to generalise but of those who responded to this question the vast majority (only 2 exceptions) encourage an inclusive approach to worship in multi-faith/no-faith situations.

(ii) There is a recognition that the word 'worship' has to bear a broader definition than given to it in Circular 1/94 to include 'stillness, silence', etc.

(iii) There was little emphasis on worship as a derivative of 'worthship'. Only one response spoke of 'things of worth' although others did refer to the sharing of beliefs, values, achievements, etc.

How can headteachers who are responsible for the administration and organisation of school worship be best assisted in their task by the diocese, the General Synod's Board of Education and the National Society?

Most responses referred to the predictable but nonetheless important:

- 'effective use of LEA and Diocesan Advisers;
- SACRES to take a more positive role in training;
- better and more in-service training;
- more effective dissemination of good practice;
- governor training;
- development of specialist RE Resource Centres'.

As pointed out earlier, a number of LEAs (and dioceses) have produced very effective guidance and support for teachers leading and organising school worship. RE resource centres, where they exist, are full of books on primary and secondary school worship; all of which have a variety of ideas.

The issue rarely addressed is the above suggestion on how to ensure that headteachers take collective school worship sufficiently seriously to ensure that staff time and money is allocated for training and that further money is available to purchase material resources. Primary-school teachers, in general, are more amenable to attending in-service training courses on school worship; secondary-school teachers, in general, are more resistant. There has to be a change of will within schools and LEAs and the Government itself if the many opportunities for in-service training are to be taken up particularly in secondary schools.

Dioceses also suggested closer links with clergy training and continuing ministerial education so that clergy would be available to offer help and support to schools. One Diocesan Board suggested that compulsory modules on school worship should be part of initial teacher training for all primary-school teachers and secondary RE specialists. The latter suggestion would not find favour with many secondary RE specialists who, in recent years, have sought to distance themselves from collective school worship. One might argue however that modules on school worship should be part of all ITT, primary and secondary.

It is also difficult to 'disseminate good practice' for this often results in another book and as one diocese pointed out:

> Just one more assembly book, however, would not appear to the Board to be the answer to a perceived difficulty.

Good practice so often depends upon the practitioner, and what passes for good practice in one situation by one person may not make the grade elsewhere. It is, however, possible that a framework for good practice can be established by LEAs, dioceses, General Synod's Board of Education and the National Society. This could be the 'good practice' of ensuring that courses are organised, money is available, school worship is seen to be an important aspect of the pupils' development, governors are made aware of their own responsibilities, and that policy-making in-servicing training is available. Some dioceses referred to the training of denominational inspectors as contributing to a deeper understanding of school worship and its possibilities in schools. Another suggested that the National Society and the General Synod's Board of Education offer national guidelines on school worship for both county and church schools (the latter it has done, in effect, through a series of publications including *Open the Door,* published jointly with the Oxford Diocesan Education Services Ltd (1994) and the National Society's *Inspection Handbook* (1995).

Finally, one or two dioceses suggested working closely with teacher organisations to ensure that progress is co-ordinated and the teacher organisations themselves will support effective training.

Summary

(i) The need to ensure that good initial and in-service training is available for teachers and clergy;

(ii) the dissemination of good practice is important but those responsible for planning and practice need to be aware of, and encouraged to use, the many books and other resources available for teachers of all age ranges;

(iii) all organisations, SACRES, unions, churches and other religious bodies should work together to ensure that schools can offer the best possible opportunities for school worship;

(iv) General Synod's Board of Education should press the Government for money to be made available specifically to support school worship, whether it is through GEST money or specific grants to other agencies.

Does the Diocesan Board of Education believe that the guidance on collective worship in schools as contained in Circular 1/94 needs amendment? If so, in what specific respects? Please be specific.

Though one or two Boards did not answer the question in detail and four Boards believed the Circular to be in no need of amendment, a large majority expressed the view that a change or amendment in some way was necessary. There was, however, a recognition that the Circular as a whole contained much useful and helpful material.

The paragraphs that came in for most specific criticism were paragraphs 51, 56, 57, 60–66, 67, 68 and 83 though not from every diocese. (There are 155 paragraphs in the Circular.) The paragraphs receiving most attention were 57 and 63. Paragraph 50 is quoted here because it is the key paragraph in Circular 1/94 which serves to provide the basic aims of collective school worship. In spite of some criticism it appears that paragraph 50 offers a broad basis for agreement.

Paragraph 50

Aims

Collective worship in schools should aim to provide the opportunity for pupils to worship God, to consider spiritual and moral issues and to explore their own beliefs; to encourage participation and response, whether through active involvement in the presentation of worship or through listening to and joining in the worship offered; and to develop community spirit, promote a common ethos and shared values, and reinforce positive attitudes.

Paragraph 57

> 'Worship' is not defined in the legislation and in the absence of any such definition it should be taken to have its natural and ordinary meaning, That is, it must in some sense reflect something special or separate from ordinary school activities and it should be concerned with reverence or veneration paid to a divine being or power. However, worship in schools will necessarily be of a different character from worship amongst a group with beliefs in common. The legislation reflects this difference in referring to 'collective worship' rather than 'corporate worship'.

The main criticism of this paragraph was that it offers a 'too simplistic view of the nature and theology of worship'. Clearly, although the 'natural and ordinary meaning' of the word 'worship' could be taken as a starting point, it is inappropriate for schools, which are by and large not faith communities, to be constrained by a dictionary definition. The third sentence of paragraph 57 indicates there is a recognition that collective school worship will be of a 'different character' to a worshipping community but gives no guidance as to how that definition of worship, even if one accepted that definition of worship, would need to be developed to meet a rather different situation. In a county school context it would appear that 'worship' could not have 'its natural and ordinary meaning' because worship is not taking place within the context of a worshipping faith community.

> Liberation from the pre-conceived notions attached to the word 'worship' would open the prospect of a much-needed flexibility, enable the more ready affirmation of social, moral and spiritual values held in common by Christians, members of other faith communities, agnostics and atheists – and might well help Christians, with others, to feel freer to share their deepest convictions and sense of commitment...

is how one Diocesan Board responded, another simply suggested it be omitted. More positively, another suggestion was made that while 'veneration' should be retained, it should be supported by 'spiritual reflection', 'meditation', etc.

> Paragraph 57 can also be interpreted as separating collective worship from the rest of school life, rather

than attempting to help re-focus it so as to sum it up or see it from a different i.e. spiritual, perspective.

The general feeling was that by offering a definition of worship the DFE had narrowed the real opportunities and possibilities opened up by the Education Reform Act 1988. The flexibility specifically endorsed by both the Government and the churches had been lost. It was not only an unhelpful definition of worship but it failed to recognise the changed context in which worship would take place which must have an effect on the 'natural and ordinary meaning' of the word 'worship'.

Paragraph 63

> Provided that, taken as a whole, an act of worship which is broadly Christian reflects the traditions of Christian belief, it need not contain only Christian material. Section 7(1) is regarded as permitting some non-Christian elements in the collective worship without thus depriving it of its broadly Christian character. Nor would the inclusion of elements common to Christianity and one or more other religions deprive it of that character. It must, however, contain some elements which relate specifically to the traditions of Christian belief and which accord a special status to Jesus Christ.

In submissions to the draft of the Circular (Circular X/94) the attention of the DFE had already been drawn to the theological difficulties as well as the practical implications of the phrase 'a special status to Jesus Christ'. This advice was not taken up in the final version of the Circular.

A range of responses from the DBEs emphasised this point:

> People need to be reminded that Christians believe in a Trinity of God the Creator, God the Redeemer and God the Holy Spirit and this perhaps can be more freeing that some would understand.

> According a 'special status to Jesus Christ' as the only or deciding characteristic of Christian Worship is . . . restrictive and emphasises the exclusion of some pupils and staff.

This manages to be offensive to just about everybody! On the one hand it offends other faiths and on the other hand it offends many Christians who feel that Jesus' status is more than just special, it is unique.

The final sentence (of paragraph 63) is a major stumbling block.

Lengthy debate on Circular 1/94 resulted in demands from the Board for its amendment, particularly over the compulsory nature of worship and over the special status given to Jesus Christ, which it was indicated could well be a Muslim attitude as well as a Christian one.

Paragraph 63 was identified as being particularly contentious. There was concern that while the Act states that the majority of acts of worship in county schools should be 'of a broadly Christian character' and 'reflect the broad traditions of Christian belief', the Circular has gone beyond this in specifying that 'broadly Christian worship... must contain some elements of which relate specifically to the traditions of Christian belief and which accord a special status to Jesus Christ'.

The following comments sum up the general concerns about Circular 1/94 by virtually every responding diocese:

> We believe that the guidance on collective worship in schools as contained in Circular 1/94 is inappropriate, unhelpful and in many county schools impossible in practice.
>
> The National Curriculum Council published helpful guidance and wording in its document on *Spiritual and Moral Development* (1993, p.7). We suggest that their wording be retained as follows:
>
> Worship offers 'pupils opportunities to:
>
> explore and share beliefs;
> consider the importance of prayer, meditation and silence;
> consider the relevance of ideas and beliefs to their own lives;

think about the needs of others and develop a sense of community and appreciate the importance of religious beliefs to those who hold them'.

This definition is much broader and fairer and would allow County schools to enable pupils to be sensitive to what lies within the language of religion and the religious quest without demanding from pupils or teachers specific assent.

There is much of value in 1/94, but the key passages on worship seek to define too much (e.g. paragraphs 57 and 63). The point here is that while we would affirm such ideas many do not. For example those who are Buddhist cannot accept paragraph 57, and those who are Jewish are offended by paragraph 63. Doctrinal statements of this nature in a Government document are destructive of the kind of consensus which is crucial if worship is to be developed in schools. Paragraph 50, by contrast offers a broad basis for agreement. Many secular Heads would accept that some pupils will want to worship God within a school act of worship and will respect this. However the negative aspect of 1/94 is considerable.

Summary

(i) There is intense concern regarding certain passages of the Circular – some of which have not been addressed here but are more specific in character and will be referred to below.

(ii) There is also a recognition that the value of much of the Circular has been lost either because of careless drafting of a few paragraphs or because of a deliberate policy to constrain the flexibility of the Education Reform Act.

(iii) 'One possible solution is to amend section 7 of the Education Act 1988 so as to require an act which recognises the duty to promote the spiritual and moral development of pupils, but which permits that duty to be interpreted in a way appropriate for the pupils, bearing in mind their family backgrounds, ages and aptitudes.'

(Quoted from a DBE response)

(iv) 'If we are concerned with pupils' spiritual development, then there must be opportunities in every school for silence, for reflection, for learning what worship is, for experiencing and expressing awe and wonder, for that growing sense of 'the other' which is an essential key to developing spirituality. Well-organised and with a suitably planned and varied programme, the collective worship slot should be able to contribute powerfully to spiritual development.'

(Quoted from a DBE response)

(v) 'DFE Circular 1/94 needs re-examination and it was recommended that the DFE be advised to consult further with relevant parties on the issues contained within it with a view to securing a consensus on which a revision could be based. A revision of the definition of worship in the Circular was particularly needed.'

(Quoted from a DBE response)

What action should be taken by the Board of Education of the General Synod?

The responses to this question were succinct:

(i) Support teachers and dioceses in their efforts to provide appropriate high quality acts of collective worship.

(ii) Work with all interested parties to bring about legislative change at the appropriate time which will benefit the spiritual and moral development of pupils.

(iii) Work to amend paragraph 56 of Circular 1/94 as well:

It is illogical that County and Controlled schools who wish to hold occasional acts of collective worship off the school premises (and many do) are penalised for doing so in that they do not then satisfy the statutory daily act of worship which is restricted to those taking place on school premises. The law should treat all schools equally. Therefore we recommend that the last sentence of paragraph 56 is amended to read: 'County and controlled schools which also wish to hold acts of collective worship off the school premises may do so'.

(Quoted from a DBE response)

(iv) Press the Government to ensure that time spent in collective worship be counted as part of curriculum time.

3

Collective School Worship Seminars

Introduction

The Seminars, generously funded by the St Gabriel's Trust In-Service Programme and organised through the National Society, were held in London, Bristol, Birmingham, Chester and York. A list of those organisations and individuals invited to the seminars is given in Appendix A and the list of those who were able to attend in Appendix B. There were, inevitably, one or two absentees at each seminar.

There were two aims for the seminars:

(i) to assist the GS Board of Education to arrive at a policy for collective school worship;

(ii) to offer practical advice and guidance to those responsible for the organisation and administration of collective school worship.

The seminars followed the same general pattern. At each one a résumé was given of the Board of Education's process of consultation of Diocesan Boards of Education.

The first half of each seminar was concerned with a educational and theological rationale; the second half with pragmatic issues.

(i) Those present were put into groups and asked to write down what they thought 'worship' was.

(ii) Next, the same groups were asked to write down what they thought 'collective school worship' was.

(iii) Then two people in each of the seminars were invited to put forward their personal view about school worship followed by a general discussion.

(iv) In the second half of each seminar the original groups were then given a topic to discuss. The topics were the same for each of the five seminars although not every topic was necessarily discussed in detail at every seminar. They were essentially pragmatic issues:

(a) Should there be daily collective worship for every pupil?

(b) Should different advice be given for (or should even the law discriminate between) primary and secondary schools?

(c) What is the most appropriate attitude to pupils of non-Christian faiths or of no faith?

(d) Should 'worship education' be an aspect of Religious Education?

(e) How should the many problems of space, numbers, accommodation and the willingness of teachers to lead worship be addressed?

Each group reported back on aspects of its discussions in the plenary and the seminar concluded with another general discussion.

Summary of points from the seminars

Introductory points of view

Ten people contributed to this part of the seminar programme. The contributions ranged widely. Some of the key points raised are paraphrased below.

There is a law, agreed by Parliament on a free vote, to which headteachers are bound. If they do not wish to make appropriate arrangements for daily collective worship then they should not apply for headships. The law, democratically agreed, should be maintained.

The vast majority of people questioned in a survey (c 70%) wished to retain school worship. Those who object to school worship do not reflect the will of the people.

Collective school worship ensures that important aspects of the nation's religious and cultural heritage are passed on through prayers, hymns, scriptural readings, etc. The Church of England must act as the pillar of authority for it is, in effect, the spiritual aspect of the State; and should ensure the preservation of spiritual values from generation to generation. Circular 1/94 makes clear what options are available for worship. The analogy of the Church of England's baptism of babies can be used as an analogy, for just as the clergy have no right to prevent the baptism of infants, so schools have no right to prevent opportunities for pupils to worship. God and children matter more than clergy and schools.

There should be no compulsory worship at all in county schools. This assertion is based on three questions:

- Is the law sound? (What is the educational and theological rationale?)
- Is it right? (The moral argument)
- Is it useful? (The pragmatic argument).

Is the law sound?

If worship is the response of the creature to the eternal, including the whole life of the universe, and glorifies the Creator and Sustainer, then why should groups of (largely) non-religious people be forced to worship?

Most people who do worship operate within religious communities. For Christians the focal point is a 'conformation to Christ' and while the Eucharist may be the norm or focal point for most Christians it will not be so for all.

So why should schools be required to worship? Even Circular 1/94 recognises that 'worship in school is different in character' (paragraph 57) from worship within religious communities? In the life of the school, 'assembly' is worthwhile and voluntary worship should be acceptable. At the moment secondary schools are, in the main, in breach of the law because it is unreasonable not just impracticable.

Is it right?

There is a confusion between religion and morality. This appears to be based on an assumption that if one is compelled to do something one is better for it. But it is *not* possible to compel worship; in fact, that attitude makes a travesty of faith which requires acceptance. This argument must stand upon integrity. Pupils should not be forced to worship and when there are pupils from different faith communities present the issues are even more complex.

Is it useful?

It is good for schools to gather together – one could use the analogy of the wedding or the funeral for a family. There will be the chance for pupils to become familiar with traditional hymns and prayers; but is this merely 'folk religion'? Should education policy be built upon it? Does it enrich the pupils educational experience? Is there any evidence to indicate that collective school worship (as opposed to 'assemblies') is viewed in a positive light by pupils and teachers?

There needs to be a distinction between school worship and RE. The latter is a core subject and 'worship education' should be a part of RE. If 'worship education' did take place in RE then there would be every opportunity for pupils to be exposed to exemplar acts of worship which could, if the pupils wished, lead on to voluntary worship. Schools would then be bringing pupils to the threshold of worship and compulsory school worship would not be necessary.

The two arguments paraphrased above were argued forcefully, but though they might be seen to represent opposite ends of the spectrum neither argument found much support among those attending the seminars. Most of the debate centred on the middle ground – how to improve the quality of pupil experience, the frequency of school worship, etc.

One of these concerns developed by another speaker, and expressed in a letter from a headteacher, part of which is quoted below, picks up something of the flavour of the argument above:

> While giving high priority to values, some schools will of course feel that values need not be derived from Christian principles, or would argue that in a pluralist society values based on Christianity will be discarded if the religious belief is discarded. Nevertheless, most schools have been content to provide 'assemblies' according to the 1944 Act. Many of us feel that if the law used the term 'assembly', as it has been called in schools, the current difficulties could have been avoided. For many Christian teachers like myself, the concept of 'collective mainly Christian worship' is a perhaps 'wholly unchristian' concept. It is only recent attempts, particularly associated with OFSTED inspections, to set aside the idea of 'assembly', redefine more precisely 'collective worship' and insist unrealistically on the literal interpre-

tation of a 50-year-old law, which has forced schools into a difficult position.

Though I speak from an evangelical theological viewpoint, I feel that those extreme conservative evangelicals who are among those most strongly pressing for a return to Christian assemblies, do *not* understand the issues. They would probably regard use of such new language a watering-down of traditional belief. They are nevertheless mistaken in expecting schools to carry out a mission in which the churches have in recent years largely failed. Moreover, if the extreme view prevailed and a simplistic return to traditional Christian assemblies was required, far greater numbers of pupils and staff would feel unable to participate...

One speaker was concerned that worship provided by schools should be of 'quality'. Pupils may encounter Jesus Christ (cf. paragraph 63 of Circular 1/94) but not at the expense of integrity or be exposed to events which might 'dishonour God'.

There were a number of other concerns:

Circular 1/94 encourages a contradiction between the 'veneration of a divine being' and the worship of that divine being by pupils from different backgrounds. What is a 'broadly Christian' God? Is this not sacrilegious? School worship is often conducted in an inappropriate atmosphere and there must be an unease about the use of the currently fashionable 'collective spirituality'. The law is not working in secondary schools and appears to be a meaningless ritual; teachers have been antagonised by Circular 1/94 and the OFSTED criteria. Then there is the spectacle of Christians dismembering each other in public over school worship. This surely dishonours God.

What could be done? There are five possibilities:

(i) Amend Circular 1/94 to resolve the contradiction and modify the definition of 'worship'. School worship should be affirmed where possible.

(ii) The law should be changed to reduce the frequency of collective worship in secondary schools (cf. the position in Scotland of an act of worship per month).

(iii) Encourage the participation of all with integrity and the creation of attitudes which inform the language, ethos and variety of format.

(iv) Involve in school worship local Christians who will be able to encourage and resource a school.

(v) There is a fear of change, a fear that all will be lost; if school worship is to go forward then the extreme views – on both sides – have to be set aside and the middle ground recaptured.

Several of those introducing the discussion touched on issues already raised above. Other speakers included one very practical example of what a school did, how it planned and prepared worship and how it was recorded.

One speaker from a teaching union indicated that teachers in the union had made it very clear that they did not wish to break the law, nor did they like doing so, but felt it was impossible to keep it to the letter. They (the teachers) would be much happier if the act of collective worship could be regarded as part of the general support provided for the spiritual and moral development of pupils rather than be regarded as a legal requirement as is the case at present.

Two speakers looked at the act of worship through the eyes of differing religions and a plural society. The issue of divisiveness was raised and the psychological significance for pupils from non-Christian faiths having to opt out, i.e. either having to make a negative statement or simply acquiesce in the mainstream. Was it not unchristian for the school system to be used manipulatively to cut across the integrity of pupil and teacher? While this discussion centred on county schools, was there no relevance for Church voluntary schools where there were members of other faith communities?

There is a lack of clarity over the purpose of collective school worship. Is it there to:

(i) Develop spiritual and moral values?

(ii) Reinforce individual faith attachment?

(iii) Induce membership of a community regardless of, or contrary to, the faith background of the pupil?

'So what', asked one speaker, 'was the original vision?'. Was it intended to be the link between worship and spirituality? Would that now be best achieved by repealing Section 7 of the Education Reform

Act and leaving Section 6, but using 'assembly' to promote the spiritual growth of the pupils and the ethos of the school? Schools should be free to draw upon the wealth of spiritual presence within their school. Surely any use of theology should be liberating and the application of theology to the issue of collective school worship should enable schools to fulfil the pupils' spiritual development far more effectively than the cramping style envisaged in Circular 1/94? Precision is unhelpful in this case, the legal situation is impossible so there is, it appears, political stalemate.

Summary of comments from the discussions

The lack of clarity regarding the law and the unease over its implementation meant that discussion often followed an elliptical route. Generally, as with the responses from the Diocesan Board of Education, there was a reluctance to change the law because it was not clear, for some, what should be put in place.

There were, however, trenchant criticisms of certain paragraphs in Circular 1/94. Referring to paragraph 57 one member noted the 'theological imperialism' of the Government usurping definitions of worship. Another expressed amazement that paragraph 63 was so theologically naive and questioned why a 'one nation' government document should refer to the messiahship of Jesus, as this was certain to inflame and cause offence.

There was further criticism of the Circular for its vague reference to pupils taking part (paragraph 59) and pupils 'who do not come from Christian families (being) able to join in the daily act of collective worship even though this would, in the main, reflect the broad traditions of Christian belief ' (paragraph 65). It would be difficult, given the narrow reference to 'Jesus Christ' in paragraph 63 to see how the intention of paragraph 65 could be fulfilled.

The guidance from OFSTED had moved more to 'inward reflection'. Should schools write their policy for school worship, noting the difficulty (or impossibility) of meeting the daily requirement, emphasising the importance of supporting pupils' spiritual and moral development? By sharing the policy and the problems of the legal requirements with governors, parents and local communities, the school, and the community it served, could reach some agreement: while the law may not be fulfilled in the letter, the school would have the support of the community or communities, which contributed to be life of the school.

There had never been a clear statement from the Government as to why collective worship was not considered to be part of the curriculum time. This was a common theme in the seminars. It was felt that if collective worship was to be educational then it had to be part of directed time. One view was that if worship was to be defined so narrowly then it could *not* be part of directed time as it was impossible of fulfilment.

The furore over the collective worship clauses in the Education Reform Act 1988 had died down. LEAs, with Church and other religious bodies, had provided very helpful support for schools. It had been recognised that the 1988 Act did allow this flexibility but that flexibility had been removed by Circular 1/94, or at the very least undermined.

The current fashion to adopt a phrase such as 'collective spirituality' was alluring but it simply encouraged vagueness and lacked rigour, but then, perhaps vagueness was preferable to the strictures of the Circular.

A recurring theme throughout the seminars was the desire for pupils to develop a sense of liturgy and be provided with a rich and varied diet of religious language and imagery, scripture, poetry and music which would (or could) support them into adult life. If the law were changed, this could be weakened. This opinion was endorsed by a number of participants who *did* wish to change the law, but it was pointed out that the above opinion implied a quality of provision which was not currently present.

There was a danger of Christians exploiting privilege and acting irresponsibly with the result of creating a fractured and divided society. Britain may be a Christian country but was it Christian for racist, nationalist or religious reasons?

Contrary to the opinion above regarding 'folk religion', it was argued that parents *do* want collective worship, and why shouldn't 'folk religion' (however defined) be acceptable? Why should the Church of England create a 'high walls' policy of what the Church is?

Initial teacher training should include modules on the preparation for, and leading of, collective worship in *all* schools for all students.

Issues Raised in the Working Groups

Worship

The work done by the groups on worship and collective school worship can not be summarised effectively. The general tenor of all the groups, however, is that worship, in the *corporate* sense is to do with the Creator-created relationship; it is to do with the nature of the Divine and the response of the created. Worship involves a God in whom the worshippers have a personal faith and to whom they make a personal response.

Collective school worship

Much of what has been referred to already occurs again here. It was pointed out that although there is a lack of clarity about the meaning of the phrase, a lot of material from 'worship' (above) was repeated in this second activity. This may indicate that the traditional division between 'collective' and 'corporate' is meaningless because the person leading worship is always unaware of what is actually taking place in the minds of those present, whether it is corporate or collective worship. In other words, regardless of the intention of the 1944 and 1988 Acts, pupils *themselves* do not make a distinction between corporate and collective worship.

What *has* become clear from the seminars is that the management of collective school worship is of a lower order than the theological, philosophical and educational rationale. It is far more important that pupils develop a language which will open up to them the insights of the great thinkers, leaders and founders of religion, help them develop an insight into the forms and patterns of worship; be able to find words and practices that will help them express joy, thanksgiving, sadness, etc. than whether collective school worship takes place daily for every pupil.

Although the word 'God' is sufficient for those Christians who believe, it clearly poses problems for members of some other faiths and agnostics and atheists. It may help if, rather than use the 'natural and ordinary meaning' of worship, school collective worship has as one of its aims to develop an awareness and/or a sense of the transcendent; something that lies beyond the mundane and something that through reflection, meditation, etc. reveals a deeper aspect of life to pupils. For some this will be God, for others it may be a moment of insight when the spirit is lifted and they see more clearly. This would hardly take place every day! But pupils should have the opportunity to experience that awareness of the transcendent some time in their lives.

In spite of observations that daily collective school worship was really only an issue in secondary schools, the general opinion within the seminars was that there should not be a different legal requirement for primary and secondary schools. There should be, however, different advice and there did need to be a change in the law. One proposal was that governors should, with the headteacher, devise their own policy on school worship within the broad framework of the 1988 Act. If worship were not to be daily for all pupils, the county schools would then ask their SACRE for dispensation to hold the act of worship less frequently. SACRE could then decide. This would provide a legal framework within which local conditions and local autonomy could apply. The law could still *prefer* daily worship with exceptions allowed through the SACRE in specific cases as so long as reasons were given and accepted by governors, parents and the SACRE.

With regard to worship in multi-faith schools there was general agreement that pupils should not be made to feel any pressure to worship a God in whom they did not believe. School worship should be 'child aware not child centred' in the sense that teachers would need to be aware of the religious background of their pupils, especially the very young pupils. Pupils should be willing to sit and listen without feeling pressure to join in. As they grow older pupils may be challenged by what they hear. This would form a positive part of their educational and spiritual development. There did appear to be an unease about multi-faith worship for two reasons:

(a) there was a theological complexity not recognised by many teachers and pupils;

(b) it could lead to a form of syncretism unacceptable to many.

There was a strong feeling that school worship (and perhaps all worship) is not a finished product. School worship provides a 'range of opportunities and insights which work towards....' So the role of music, dance, gesture, prayer, singing, etc. make up part of the core knowledge and skills of worship itself. In other words collective school worship has an educative function which, while not trespassing on the sacred ground of each person, should be pressing in on the fringes of that ground. 'Theology should be liberating', someone had said, so too perhaps, should worship.

4

Conclusion

Current and future action

The central concern of the Board, and it is shared by DBEs, other churches, unions, etc. is that of quality. In primary schools it appears about 85% of schools are able, according to inspection evidence, to meet the legal daily requirement. There is not considered to be any need for change. But what of the quality of worship? What about the qualifications of teachers to lead or plan worship? What about the school policy? In secondary schools where only about 20% *do* keep the legal requirement (and that includes voluntary schools) surely the same issue of quality is central. The legal obligation should be a subsidiary issue to the quality on offer.

Although schools may well be anxious to be seen to keep to the law, the main concern of most of those consulted was that each act of worship should be of good quality and that school polices should offer pupils a wide range of opportunities.

The opinion in the DBEs and expressed in the seminars, though not with unanimity, was that while it was desirable that secondary schools should keep the law and make every effort to do so, it was more important that the schools' policies on spiritual and moral development be seen to be in place and judged to be effective.

What is required most urgently is an act of political will, not in Parliament, or at least not yet, but in schools. Governors, headteachers and staff need to recognise that if the act of worship can be allowed a freedom, a liberation, from the narrow framework found in some paragraphs of Circular 1/94 then it can contribute directly and purposefully to the spiritual and moral development of all their pupils. Many schools, especially secondary schools, do not have that political will, and yet as one headteacher wrote:

> *Headteachers* 'share wholeheartedly the wish to inculcate values, to emphasise the corporate nature of the school community, and the need for schools to give moral and spiritual leadership in a society which has fewer and

fewer shared values. Schools may be one of the few centres of civilised values available to their community.... Schools are therefore as aware as the Church of the need to strengthen shared values and principles.'

What does the OFSTED handbook require?

The following extracts are taken from the OFSTED handbook, *Guidance on the Inspection of Nursery and Primary Schools,* published in October 1995. The same information appears in *Guidance on the Inspection of Secondary Schools,* pp. 88–93, also published in October 1995.

In the guidance for inspection of spiritual, moral, social and cultural development, attention is drawn to the importance of creating a wide range of opportunities for pupils:

> Overall judgements are concerned with the opportunities given for pupils to learn about and explore different values, beliefs and views and to develop and express their own. Judgements should be based on evidence from the whole curriculum and the day-to-day life of the school, including the examples set by adults and the quality of collective worship. This is an area on which evidence must be drawn from all members of the team before considered corporate judgements are made. The judgements are best made in conjunction with those on other aspects of provision.
>
> *('Inspection focus', p. 83)*

> Effective provision for spiritual development... depends on a curriculum and approaches to teaching which embody clear values and enable pupils to gain understanding through reflection on their own and other people's lives and beliefs, and their environment. It relies on teachers receiving and valuing pupils' ideas across the whole curriculum, for example, in stories, in pupils' writing, art, music, history and in religious education.... Acts of collective worship play a particular part. To the extent that spiritual insights imply an awareness of how pupils relate to others, there is a strong link to both moral and social development.
>
> *('Using the criteria', p. 83)*

Inspection of acts of collective worship is needed in all schools which do not provide denominational education except in nursery schools. Evaluation should focus on whether acts of worship are well planned and encourage pupils to explore questions about meaning and purpose, values and beliefs. Compliance with statutory requirements on collective worship should be reported.

('Using the criteria', pp. 83–4)

Of collective worship, the following guidance is given:

> The law requires schools, other than nursery schools and pupil referral units, to provide a daily act of collective worship. Taken over a term, the majority of such acts of worship should be wholly or mainly of a broadly Christian character. The school prospectus should make clear parents' right to withdraw their children from collective worship. Defining worship is difficult because a wide a variety of activities is used by people of all faiths. In forming a judgement about the character and quality of worship in schools, the following points may be helpful:
>
> - worship is generally understood to imply the recognition of a supreme being. It should be clear that the words used and/or the activities observed in worship recognise the existence of a deity;
>
> - much that is identifiably Christian in tone, may not necessarily mention Jesus. This is true of some hymns and prayers used regularly as part of worship within Christian churches. However, if the worship consistently avoids reference to Jesus within the spoken or written word then it could not reasonably be defined as mainly Christian;
>
> - collective worship should not be judged by the presence of a particular ingredient. It might include: sharing values of a Christian narture; opportunities for prayers or meditation; opportunities to reflect upon readings from holy texts or other writings which bring out religious themes; performance of music, drama and/or dance;

- each act of worship in a school should be considered as a piece. Before reaching a judgement the activities observed during the inspection should be set alongside the evidence of what has occurred, and is planned, over a term. If on balance it is judged that what the school provides is not in keeping with the spirit of the law, then this should be recorded and the reason(s) given. (Section 6.1 covers non-compliance with statutory requirements);

- worship may be judged not to fulfil statutory requirements but could still be observed to make a powerful contribution to spiritual, moral, social and cultural development. That should be made clear in the report.

(Additional notes, 'Collective worship', p.87)

Inspectors are reminded of their responsibilities:

> ... The inspection team should inspect acts of worship, except in schools where collective worship falls to be inspected under Section 13 of the 1992 Act or where collective worship is not required.
>
> *(p.13, paragraph 21)*

The approach taken in the guidance appears to emphasise the importance of the spiritual and moral development of pupils and to place the daily legal requirement to a subsidiary position. Inspectors are to report on whether the daily legal requirement is met, but greater emphasis appears to be laid upon the responsibility of the whole school to promote the spiritual, moral, social and cultural development of pupils across the whole curriculum and in school life generally. The notes under 'Collective worship' reflect the intention of Circular 1/94 while avoiding those passages which are regarding by some as being the most contentious.

Churches Joint Education Policy Committee

The Churches Joint Education Policy Committee (CJEPC) produced a consultative document which as been used as background reading for the seminars. It is not intended to reproduce the whole document here but Section 5 of the document, 'Theological aspects of collective worship', is included in Appendix D as it encapsultates some of the main theological issues raised in the continuing debate on school worship.

The CJEPC document lends force to the argument that paragraph 57 in Circular 1/94 is not only too simplistic, it does not even begin to address the nature of worship when that worship is constrained by a school context.

The Religious Education Council

This body, with members from various organisations with an interest in RE, is to set up an examination of the role and place of school worship continuing the current momentum. The Inter-Faith Network and the National Association of SACRES is to join the REC in reflecting the interest of faith groups as well as those primarily concerned with education.

Conclusion

So, if that is the current situation, what needs to be done? At a governmental level it appears there will be no immediate change in the law, although the current Secretary of State has been very quiet on the subject of RE and worship. It may be that the swirls and eddies that lie beneath the surface suggest the need to establish clearer objectives both in terms of any specific legal changes and identification of what 'collective school worship' means.

Unfortunately the very tenor of certain paragraphs in Circular 1/94 means that the DfEE is committed to a stance strongly advised against by many, including some of the churches. It will be difficult for them to change. The limitations of paragraphs 57 and 63 indicate the problem of the State becoming too deeply involved in the detail of theology.

Publications from the Board (in 1984), and more recent publications from the National Society, many dioceses and LEAs, provide an enormous range of support for teachers. It is not enough to disseminate good practice; the good practice of one teacher using material selected to suit their own approach and interest together with the material being presented in a very personal style does not always easily translate to other teachers in other schools. There are plenty of worship (assembly) books and as one DBE remarked the 'answer is not another assembly book'.

5

The Board of Education – A Policy Statement: School Worship

he Board believes collective worship is an entitlement for pupils which contributes significantly to their spiritual and moral development.

Introduction

The Board of Education has listened carefully to the wide range of opinion expressed during its consultation with Diocesan Boards of Education and in the seminars that took place under the auspices of the National Society. No Diocesan Board voted for the abolition of collective worship in county schools, although individuals on some Boards were of that view.

There is, however, some dissatisfaction with the law as it stands, particularly with the requirements that every registered pupil should attend a daily act of collective worship (unless withdrawn by the parents.) This unease expresses itself most clearly through the responses of the Diocesan Boards of Education and especially in relation to secondary schools but there is no unanimity on what should be put in place of the daily requirement.

Many voices in both the seminars and the Diocesan Boards of Education pointed out the anomaly that worship for the county and voluntary controlled school, if held in a church, did not 'count' as collective worship and other services had to be arranged on the same day in the school (cf. Circular 1/94, paragraph 56).

Much of the discontent is not with primary legislation formulated in the 1988 Education Act. It appears to be rooted in three or four paragraphs of Circular 1/94, 'Religious education and collective worship', notably paragraphs 57, 59, 63 and 65. These paragraphs have been accepted by OFSTED as forming part of the basic criteria to be used when inspecting collective school worship in county schools. The Board is concerned that some evident dissatisfaction with some aspects of Circular 1/94 may lead to a diminution of the overall quality of acts of worship.

The Board is of the view that if the DfEE were to indicate how flexible the primary legislation is *and* be prepared to offer supplementary guidance to Circular 1/94 reinforcing that flexibility, then much of the anxiety would be removed from the situation. Schools would be able to plan more effectively how best to provide for the spiritual development of their pupils in collective worship within the context of their own local communities.

The Policy of the Board on Collective School Worship

(i) In the light of all the evidence and opinion, the Board's own carefully considered opinion is that collective worship should be maintained in schools as part of the pupil's educational experience.

(ii) The Board does not wish, at the present time, to press for a change in the law on the daily requirement for school worship. It regards the present law as providing a sufficient framework within which schools can explore effective forms of worship.

(iii) The Board does, however, recognise that an argument has been made for change in the legislation as applied to the daily provision of worship. The Board, therefore, wishes to continue purposeful discussions with the DfEE, OFSTED and other interested parties, including other churches and other faith communities, in order to work towards an acceptable agreed framework for collective worship.

(iv) The Board encourages schools to adopt a policy for worship broadly based on paragraph 50 of Circular 1/94 and to share their policies on collective worship and spiritual and moral development with parents and members of the communities served by the school.

(v) It is the view of the Board that the paragraphs of Circular 1/94, which many regard as contentious (particularly numbers 57, 59, 63 and 65), confuse the policy and purpose of the 1988 Education Reform Act. The Board welcomes the clarification on the law provided in the October 1995 edition of the OFSTED handbook.

(vi) In addition to the proposed discussions, the Board continues to encourage governors, headteachers and teachers to support the spiritual and moral development of pupils with particular regard to the appointment of staff and the commitment of resources.

(vii) The Board would welcome clarification from the DfEE as to why collective school worship is not regarded as curriculum time.

(viii) The Board looks to the TTA and those institutions responsible for initial teacher training, to ensure that proper training is available for students in the management and conduct of school worship.

(ix) The Board urges the DfEE to provide specific funds for the in-service training of teachers who are required to lead or manage acts of collective school worship.

(x) The Board is most concerned that when Church voluntary controlled schools hold a service in church during the school day this is not regarded as collective worship. The Board urges the Government to amend the law in this specific case. This would bring the situation for controlled schools into line with the law regarding aided and special agreement schools.

(xi) The Board suggests that the DfEE, with appropriate consultation, considers the general case for any act of worship off the premises of county schools to be regarded as the act of collective worship.

(xii) The Board calls upon Diocesan Boards of Education and ecumenical partners to accept greater responsibility for the support and enhancement of collective worship in all schools through their in-service courses for teachers and clergy and resource centres.

Appendix A

School Worship Seminars: Those Invited to Attend

The General Synod Board of Education
The GS Board of Education Schools' Committee
The GS Board of Education Curriculum Advisory Group/RE Working Party
15 Diocesan Directors of Education
22 Diocesan RE Advisers
The Department for Education
OFSTED
SCAA
Baptist Union
Catholic Services in Education
Free Church Federal Council
Methodist Division of Education and Youth
United Reformed Church
The Bloxham Project
Christian Education Movement
Christians in Education
The Christian Institute
The Church Society
Council of Christians and Jews
Evangelical Alliance
The Interfaith Network
The Order of Christian Unity
The Church College Trusts
Representatives from HE Colleges
Association of Anglican Secondary School Headteachers
Association of Christian Teachers
Association of Jewish Teachers
Catholic Teachers Federation
National Association of Standing Advisory Councils for Religious Education
Professional Council for Religious Education
The Religious Education Council
The Grant Maintained Schools Foundation
The Independent Schools Information Service

Association of Teachers and Lecturers
The National Association of Head Teachers
National Association of Schoolmasters/Union of Women Teachers
National Union of Teachers
The Professional Association of Teachers
Secondary Heads Association
National Confederation of Parent-Teacher Associations
The Revd Dr John Gay, Culham College Institute
Professor John Hull, University of Birmingham
The Revd Canon Christopher Lamb, GS Board of Mission
Dr Andrew Purkis, Lambeth Palace
The Revd Derek Webster, University of Hull
Members of other faith communities:
    Baha'i
    Dr Stephen Vickers
    Buddhist
    Mr Anil Goonewardene
    Mr Ron Maddox, Buddhist Society
    Hindu
    Mr Dilip Kadodwala
    Mr Deepak Naik, National Council of Hindu Temples
    Rasamandala Das, ISKCON
    Jain
    Mr Vinod Kapashi
    Jewish
    Ms Angela Wood, SCIFDE
    Mr Laurie Rosenberg, Board of Deputies of British Jews
    Mrs Sally Strauss, Association of Jewish Teachers
    Rabbi Hugo Gryn, West London Synagogue
    Syma Weinburg, Jewish Education Development Trust
    Muslim
    Mr Mohammed Akram Khan Cheema, Muslim Education Forum
    Mr Ibrahim Hewitt, Association of Muslim Schools
    Mr Muhammad Ibrahim, Muslim Educational Trust
    Dr Abdul Mabud, The Islamic Academy
    Mr Nazar Mustafa, Muslim Education Co-ordinating Council
    Mr Yousif Al-Khoei, Al-Khoei Foundation
    Mr Umar Hegedus, AMANA
    Sikh
    Sardar Harcharan Singh Dua, Sikh Cultural Society
    Kanwaljit Singh Kaur
    Manjit Kaur

Appendix B

School Worship Seminars: Those Expected to Attend*

London: Wednesday, 17th May 1995

Chairman: The Rt Revd the Lord Bishop of Ripon
Chairman of The National Society and of The General Synod Board of Education

The Revd David Adlington, Diocesan Director of Education, Llandaff
Mr Alan Brown, Schools Officer (RE), GS Board of Education; Deputy Director, The National Society; Director, The National Society's RE Centre
Mr Terry Brown, GS Board of Education/National Society Curriculum Advisory Group
Mr Michael Catty, Association of Teachers and Lecturers
Dr Owen Cole, London Diocesan Board for Schools/Council of Churches for Britain and Ireland/Education Group
Ms Anita Compton, London Diocesan Board for Schools
Mrs Margaret Dean, RE Adviser, Guildford Diocesan Board of Education
Mrs Geraldine Everett, Professional Association of Teachers
Ms Naomi Franks, Association of Jewish Teachers
Ms Samidha Garg, National Union of Teachers Race Equality
Ms Erica Haige, Council of Christians and Jews
The Revd Canon Peter Hartley, GS Board of Education/The National Society Curriculum Advisory Group and Diocesan Director of Education, Chelmsford
Mr Umar Hegedus, AMANA
Mrs Ann Holt, CARE
Mr Roy Hughes, GS Board of Education/The National Society Curriculum Advisory Group
Ms Rosemary Johnston, United Reformed Church
The Revd John Joyce, Diocesan Director of Education, Chichester
Dr Shaikh Abdul Mabud, The Islamic Academy
Professor Arthur Pollard, GS Board of Education
Dr Andrew Purkis, Lambeth Palace
Mr L S Rosenberg, Board of Deputies of British Jews
Mrs Alison Seaman, Deputy Director, The National Society's RE Centre

Mr David Trainor HMI, OFSTED
Mrs Lilian Weatherley, Diocesan RE Adviser, Winchester
Miss Mary Williams, RE Adviser, Southwark Diocesan Board of Education
Mr George Wiskin, National Union of Teachers

York: Monday, 22nd May 1995

Chairman: The Rt Revd the Lord Bishop of Ripon
Chairman of The National Society and The General Synod Board of Education

Mrs Janina Ainsworth, RE Adviser, Manchester Diocesan Board of Education
Mr John Bailey, Diocesan Director, Lincoln Diocesan Board of Education
Mr Alan Brown, Schools Officer (RE), GS Board of Education; Deputy Director,
    The National Society; Director, The National Society's RE Centre
Mr Mark Chater, Bishop Grosseteste College
Mr David K Edwards, RE Adviser, Birmingham Diocesan Board of Education
Mr Michael Evans, Association of Anglican Secondary School Headteachers
The Revd Gerry Forster, RE Adviser, Newcastle Diocesan Board of Education
The Revd Malcolm Foy, RE Adviser, Ripon Diocesan Board of Education
Professor Leonard Marsh, Bishop Grosseteste College
Mrs Alison Seaman, Deputy Director and Resources Officer, The National
    Society's RE Centre, London
The Revd Derek Webster, University of Hull
Mrs Deirdre Wilmore, RE Adviser, Derby Diocesan Board of Education
Mr Ian Wragg HMI, OFSTED
Mrs Brenda Willis, Churches Commission on Interfaith Dialogue

Chester: Wednesday, 31st May 1995

Chairman: The Revd Canon Alan Nugent
Chairman of the Diocesan Directors of Education

The Revd Canon Roger Bird, Diocesan Director of Education, St Asaph
Mr Alan Brown, Schools Officer (RE), GS Board of Education; Deputy Director,
    The National Society; Director, The National Society's RE Centre
Mrs Erica Brown, GS Board of Education, Schools' Committee
Dr Trevor Cooling, Association of Christian Teachers
Mr Jack Davies, Church in Wales Provincial Schools Consultant
The Revd Canon John Eardley, Diocesan Director of Education, Coventry
Ms Joan Furlong, RE Adviser, Diocese of Lichfield
Miss Jane Griffiths, GS Board of Education/National Socicty Curriculum Advisory
    Group
The Revd John Hall, Diocesan Director of Education, Blackburn

Ms Manjit Kaur, Coventry LEA/SACRE Vice Chair
The Revd Mike Ranyard, RE Adviser, Diocesan Board of Education
The Revd Peter Shepherd, Association of Anglican Secondary School
 Headteachers and GS Board of Education/National Society Curriculum
 Advisory Group
The Revd John Smith, RE Adviser, Southwell Diocesan Board of Education

Bristol: Tuesday, 6th June 1995

Chairman: The Revd Canon Rex Chapman
Chairman of the GS Board of Education's Schools' Committee

Mrs Margaret Behenna, Diocesan Director of Education, Exeter
Mr Alan Brown, Schools Officer (RE) GS Board of Education; Deputy Director,
 The National Society; Director, The National Society's RE Centre
Mr Mike Brownbill, RE Adviser, Diocese of Bath and Wells
Mrs Pauline Day, National Society Standing Committee
Mrs Daphne Griffith, GS Board of Education
Ms Amanda Haehner, NAS/UWT
Mr Henry Head, Diocesan Director of Education, Salisbury
Mr Peter Harvey, CAFOD
Professor John Hull, University of Birmingham
Mr Tristram Jenkins, Diocesan Director of Education, Hereford
The Revd Richard Lindley, Diocesan Director of Education, Birmingham
Mr Nazar Mustapha, Muslim Education Co-ordinating Council
Dr Vanessa Parffrey, University of Exeter
The Revd Canon Robin Protheroe, Diocesan Director of Education, Bristol
Mr Derek Robson, Methodist Church
Mr Michael Spinks, Chelmsford Diocesan Board of Education and Training

Birmingham: Thursday, 15th June 1995

Chairman: The Revd Canon Rex Chapman
Chairman of the GS Board of Education's Schools' Committee

Mrs Janina Ainsworth, RE Adviser, Diocese of Manchester
Mr Latymer Blaylock, Professional Council for RE
Mr Alan Brown, Schools Officer (RE), GS Board of Education; Deputy Director,
 The National Society; Director, The National Society's RE Centre
The Revd Gregory Cameron, The Bloxham Project
The Revd Richard Cheetham, Diocese of St Albans
Ms Sheila Dainton, Association of Teachers and Lecturers
Mr Colin Hart, The Christian Institute

Mr Ibrahim Hewitt, Association of Muslim Schools
Mr W G Hordern, Birmingham Diocesan Synod and SACRE
The Revd Canon Michael Ipgrave, GS Council for Interfaith Relations
Mr Dilip Kadodwala, National Association of Standing Advisory Councils on Religious Education
Mr Sayyed Nadeem Kazmi, Al-Khoei Foundation
Mr Depak Naik, The National Council of Hindu Temples
Mr Brian Pearce, Interfaith Network
Mrs Margaret Sedgwick, RE Adviser Coventry Diocesan Board of Education
Mr Dudley Shipton, National Association of Head Teachers
Ms Linda Trost, RE Adviser, Leicester Diocesan Board of Education
Mr Andrew Turner, Grant Maintained Schools Foundation
Ms Anne Young, RE Adviser, Wakefield Diocesan Board of Education

* *Owing to circumstances a number of people who indicated they wished to attend were unavailable on the day.*

Appendix C

School Worship: Invitation from the Board of Education

General Synod's Board of Education invited all Diocesan Boards of Education to discuss the following questions and to respond by 30th June 1995.

The General Synod's Board of Education made the following statement last year:

> The Board of Education is keenly aware of, sensitive to and challenged by the concerns of Headteachers, teachers and others on the issue of School worship. It believes that more work needs to be done in the area and intends to:
>
> i) encourage dioceses and other church organisations to continue to provide resources, courses and advice for those responsible for school worship;
>
> ii) invite all Diocesan Boards of Education to reflect on issues locally and report back to General Synod's Board of Education by 30th June 1995;
>
> iii) set up a series of seminars on School Worship in all primary and secondary schools with other interested parties;
>
> iv) continue with our ecumenical partners, to examine Circular 1/94 and the issues arising from it.

The Board is not, at this time, pressing for a change in the law but will review its position in the light of these consultations.

In the light of this the Diocesan Board's of Education were asked to consider the following questions, making it clear in any response whether comments made applied to County or to Church schools or to both:

1. The law requires every maintained school to provide a daily act of collective worship to be provided for every pupil registered at the school (unless withdrawn by

parental request). Would the Diocesan Board of Education agree with the law as it stands, or press or a change? What is the rationale for its opinion on this issue?

2. How best can schools meet the challenge of conducting daily worship in schools in a multi-faith/no faith community?

3. How can headteachers who are responsible for the administration and organisation of school worship be best assisted in their task by the diocese, the General Synod's Board of Education and the National Society?

4. Does the Diocesan Board of Education believe that the guidance on collective worship in schools as contained in Circular 1/94 needs amendment? If so, in what respects? Please be specific.

5. If the answer to 1 and/or 4 is 'yes' what action should be taken by General Synod's Board of Education?

Appendix D

An Extract from the CJEPC Working Party Document on Collective Worship

Theological aspects of collective worship

Collective worship is an activity designated by, and peculiar to, the law of England and Wales. It is not the same as an act of worship in a particular faith community. From a Christian perspective, the believing community (and its family members) offers, and takes part in, corporate worship through Jesus Christ. Where such a corporate body does not exist, or where Chrsitians only appear as individuals (alongside other individuals who either do not believe or are believing adherents of other religions), the worship appropriate to a Christian community is impossible. From the perspective of other faith communities, similar difficulties are to be found. The nature and diversity of the composition of the school, when collected together, therefore, poses the danger of a syncretism of the common elements of the religions represented in it, which would produce a theological model of common worship which was false to each religion. Since worship, prayer and religious meditation are always set in the context of a particular faith – its experience, history, and the implications of its terminology – it is not possible with integrity to speak of common worship. The distinctiveness of each religion is the way in which (or the Person through whom) the Transcendent is revealed.

Given this theological aspect – that proper worship is distinctive of each religion – some have argued that the only recourse for the school is to disperse contemporaneously into separate religious communities, in order to engage in particular worship. Although acknowledging, as the law also does, the right to seek a 'determination' for such separate worship, we are pleased to note that the representatives of the faith communities whom we have consulted want to preserve, but do not generally wish to emphasise, this option since it could prove divisive of the school's community and might result in undesirable consequences elsewhere within, or outside of, the school. It certainly would not be seen to be contributing to the development of the school's well-being.

The theological situation is further complicated by the fact that this document is intended to address theological aspects which have to be related to the whole age span from 5 to 18 years (and older for the staff!) and must allow for the fact that the religious insights and experiences of worship cannot neccessarily be absolutely tied to any age-related theory of child or intellectual development. The depth of a genuine experience of worship may not be at all age-related – though an articulate and rational description of it by the worshipper might be.

On the other hand, there are 'worshipful' activities in which members of the school community can engage or to which they can respond – provided that there is respect for the right of each pupil or staff member to respond or not respond, to participate actively or passively, or to 'opt out mentally'. For example, the sense of the transcendent, the awareness of the infinite and of one's position within it, the acceptance of life as given, the sense of mystery and wonder, the celebration of personal fulfilment and of those who have given service to others, the concern for the created world and for all life, the acknowledgement of moral demands – all these might provide opportunities and procedures for collective worship, provided that the leader neither gives religious offence to particular believers nor appears to require hypocritical responses from pupils and staff. Sincerity and integrity are essential in the practice of worship – and not merely in the act of believing.

There is a need, therefore, for theologians and educationalists to explore how far schools should or can produce an act of collective worship which is at the same time both 'open' for non-believers and 'closed' for believers. The law requires a majority of acts in a school to be wholly or mainly of a broadly Christian character [Education Reform Act 1988, paras. 7(1) and (3)]. Must the legal requirement of Section 7(2) 'to reflect the broad traditions of Christian belief' not only allow for the worship of the Creator God but also require pupils and staff to commit themselves to an acknowledgement of Jesus as Christ (i.e. for Christians, as Lord and Son of God), when the majority of pupils may come from homes where there is no such commitment (or they are not of an age to understand it)? Does the broadly Christian character of collective worship in schools, which certainly, according to Christian scripture, requires sincerity and a free response from those who attend, also allow for a less defined acknowledgement of Jesus which will, in schools, seek to be inclusive, rather than exclusive of some members of the community? An overt reference to God as creator and sustainer of life might in some schools be more acceptable than a public affirmation of Jesus as Son of God; but neither will be believed by all those present, given the diversity of beliefs in the family backgrounds (and cultures) which the pupils reflect. Again we note the unspecified breadth of Christian beliefs to which the Act refers; this could include a span from Roman Catholic to Society of Friends or Unitarian. Sensitivity in the use of all the language of worship is, therefore, needed if the occasions are to be educationally effective, and as broad and inclusive as possible.

But even if there is a theological case for arguing that there are some concepts and concerns which all religions address, the fact of the distinctiveness of each religion's worship means that the broadly Christian collective worshipping activity must involve, in each school term, some of the essential beliefs, events, festivities and concerns distinctive of Christianity – and as the religion dominant in British history there is a natural justification for this.

There is, however, no doubt that whatever is done on those occasions where the school tries to provide a majority of broadly Christian acts, there are tremendous opportunities to provide a balanced and broad 'diet' of variety, diversity and flexibility. The use of significant events in the history of religions (festivals, 'saints' days, the work of moral or social 'pioneers') and in the lives of secular individuals or the activities of charitable organisations, should be an opportunity not just for moral (or financial!) appeals but for challenging pupils and staff to understand and respond to such examples of excellence or humility or dedication or altrusim. In so doing the 'affective', and not merely the cognitive, aspects of religion and of education will be harnessed. Pupils will begin to appreciate not only differences between religions (and the reasons for apparently similar festivals or concerns) but also the need to embody in their own lives and in the whole life of the school and of society the highest of which the human spirit is capable.

It is clear that there is a vast resource of material and approaches in which the school (when collected together as a whole or in the year, or house, groups) can be involved without offence or hypocrisy. What is needed is for the educators, monitored and assisted by the theologians, to develop a range of suggestions and examples of good practice. For a theological study of all religions would support the view of one assessment of Christianity and of Jesus – that the highest cannot fully be spoken, it can only be acted.

A Selection of National Society Publications

Available by mail order from the National Society at the address on page 50:

Church School Inspection: A Guide for Schools of the Church of England and the Church in Wales by Lois M R Louden and David S Urwin. A practical training guide produced as a companion to *Mission, Management and Appraisal,* by the same authors. (NS £15.00)

Inspection Handbook for Section 13 Inspectors in schools of the Church of England and the Church in Wales by Alan Brown and David W Lankshear. (NS £15.00) A handbook to the whole process of inspection under Section 13 of the Education (Schools) Act 1992.

Open The Door: Guidelines for worship and for the inspection of worship in voluntary and grant-maintained Church schools by David Barton, Alan Brown and Erica Brown (NS/Oxford Diocesan Education Services, £3.00).

Church School Staffing by Lois M R Louden and David S Urwin. An essential resource for the whole process of selecting and appointing teachers, headteachers and support staff in Church schools of all kinds: aided, controlled and grant-maintained. (NS £15.00)

Available by mail order post free from the National Society (new titles issued FREE to members on publication):

School Worship (NS £1.50). For teachers and governors in Church and country schools.

The Curriculum: A Christian View (NS £1.50). A discussion of the values on which the curriculum should be based.

Primary School Worship by Alan and Eric Brown (NS £3.00). A practical guide for county, voluntary, grant-maintained and independent schools.

Opening Their Eyes: Worship and RE with Children with Special Needs by Erica Musty (Brown) (NS £1.50). Guidance for teachers in schools of all kinds.

Mixed Blessings: The Special Child in Your School by Erica Brown (NS £3.00). Advice and information for mainstream schools facing the challenges of pupils with special educational needs.

Looking for Quality in a Church School by David W Lankshear (NS £2.00). An introduction to appraisal and school inspection.

Sex Education: Guidelines for Church School Governors by Alan Brown (NS £2.00). Questions for discussion and curriculum guidelines for a potentially delicate subject.

Preparing for Inspection in a Church School by David W Lankshear (NS £2.50). Essential reading for governors, headteachers and teachers now that the new system for the inspection of maintained schools has come into operation.

Continuing in the Way: Children, Young People and the Church by Leslie J Francis and David W Lankshear (NS £1.75). A survey with important implications for the Church in the Decade of Evangelism.

In the Catholic Way (NS/The Church Union £3.00) and *In the Evangelical Way* (NS £3.00). The results of further analysis of Anglican parishes of different traditions and their contact with young people.

Small Schools by David W Lankshear (NS £3.00). An up-to-date guide for all concerned with small schools and their roles in the community.

Christianity in the Agreed Syllabus by Alan Brown (NS £2.50). An authoritative and helpful guide to RE in schools.

The Multi-Faith Church School by Alan Brown (NS £2.25). Not a contradiction in terms, but a common and encouraging reality.

Moral Education by Janina Ainsworth and Alan Brown (NS £3.00). A topical and helpful guide for both Church and county schools.

For details of application froms for teaching posts, staff contract forms, books for school and parish education and all the services provided by the National Society, please send for a free catalogue from the address on page 50.

The National Society

The National Society (Church of England) for Promoting Religious Education supports everyone involved in Christian education – teachers, school governors, students, parents, clergy, parish and diocesan education teams – with the resources of its RE centres, courses, conferences and archives.

Founded in 1811, the Society was chiefly responsible for setting up the nationwide network of Church schools in England and Wales, and still helps them with legal and administrative advice for head-teachers and governors. It was also a pioneer in teacher education through the Church colleges. The Society now provides resources for those responsible for RE and worship in any school, lecturers and students in colleges, and clergy and lay people in parish education. It publishes a wide range of books and booklets and two magazines, *Crosscurrent* (free to members) and *Together with Children*.

The National Society is a voluntary body which works in partnership with the Church of England General Synod Board of Education and the Division for Education of the Church of Wales. An Anglican society, it also operates ecumenically, and helps to promote inter-faith education and dialogue through its RE centres.

For a free resources catalogue and details of individual, corporate and associate membership contact:

>The Promotions Officer
>The National Society
>Church House
>Great Smith Street
>London SW1P 3NZ
>Telephone: 0171-222 1672
>Fax: 0171-233 2592